SHE HAS MY HAND

Dedicated to the loving memory of Heather Ann, my first baby and my sweet little angel.

Cheryl Krajcsik

CONTENTS

1. 1st Day of my Family Life………..Page 5

2. In Philadelphia …………………..Page 14

3. The Third Season of Family Life
   Back at Home…………………Page 25

4. A New Year, A New Beginning…Page 37

5. Second Chapter at Children's Hospital in
   Philadelphia………………………Page 50

6. Closing In ………………………..Page 77

7. A New Chapter in my Life ………Page 93

INTRODUCTION

In 1978 Heather Ann Wolf was born in a small local hospital in Camp Hill. The Doctors said she was perfect! Just what a new mom wanted to hear. However at exactly one month of age, I found out differently.

This book takes you through my life with her and how we worked through all types of challenges. My hope is for this book to help other moms and dads going through difficult times and daily life with special needs children. Whether it is heart disease or something else, we all need a rock to lean on. We all need to stop thinking, I couldn't do that, or I can't even imagine. Think about yourself, your children. Hug them daily and teach them your best life's lessons because you never know when they may need those strengths.

If this book helps just one family going through life raising a Chronic Heart Disease child or any other special needs child, I will have accomplished my goal.

As a result of having Heather, my husband Bob and I have created <u>Captains Sharing & Caring</u> and open our hearts and boats to special needs children all summer long on the Chesapeake Bay. Won't you join us? Relax with us on the beautiful waters and gain strength and healing from the power in those waters. Your children will be exhilarated and relaxed all at the same time, thanks to the Magic in the Water.

1ST DAY OF MY FAMILY LIFE – CHAPTER ONE

In March of 1977, I started a new chapter in my life. I got married and a new part of my adult life adventure began on September 9th, 1978. Heather Ann entered this world at ten thirty in the morning, weighing six lbs one ounce and was eighteen and one half inches long.   She was born at Holy Spirit

Hospital and was released with me on September 13th at ten thirty in the morning. Her pediatrician said she was perfect, no issues. What a relief! Heather was born in September and we had moved into our new house in August, so my life had taken a bunch of big turns all at once. But, everything appeared to be good, in fact GREAT! Until one month later.

On Monday, October 9th at seven thirty in the evening, we arrived home after a visit to grandma and grandpa's house. I put Heather in her cradle since she was sound asleep. Her cradle was on the first floor and I ran up to quickly change my clothes. When I arrived back downstairs, Heather was awake. I decided it was probably a good time to get her into her pajamas also. I picked her up from her cradle and started to change her. I noticed she seemed to be in a cold sweat. I took her temperature and it was 98 degrees. I waited a few minutes more, thinking maybe she was too warm from being bundled up on our trip home from grandmas. Her daddy ran out to the pharmacy to pick up a nasal syringe because she also seemed a bit stuffy. I also noticed she didn't seem to be breathing right, probably due to the stuffy nose. I reminded myself that new moms worry about everything and I should just try to relax. All of a sudden her eyes closed and she stopped breathing in my arms. I held her out away from my body and gently shook her. Water started to run out of her nose and ears. Where in the world was this coming from?

Of course, being a first time mom I decided to put all these things together. She was in a cold sweat, her nose was stuffy, she had fluid running out of her ears and nose, and her temp was now a little more than ninety eight degrees. My heavens what could be wrong? Her dad wasn't home yet, but I decided to call Heather's pediatrician. She was only one month old, of course I was worried and I had to call.

After I told her pediatrician everything that had happened, he told me to put Heather's mouth to the phone. Really? Put my one month old daughter's mouth to the phone? What was that going to prove? I trusted her Dr. implicitly, so I held her face close to the phone. The Dr. said <u>she is panting, how quickly can you get here</u>? We left as soon as her daddy got back and made it to the hospital in record time, which was in a different city, about thirty minutes away. By eight thirty Heathers pediatrician had admitted her and started to do some tests. The doctor did x-rays, an EKG, and then he contacted a cardiologist for Heather.

In the next several hours my world turned upside down. A cardiologist, Dr. Nordenberg, came and met with us. He said Heather had a fifty per cent chance of survival. The doctors had determined she either didn't have a left ventricle in her heart, which meant they would keep her comfortable; or she maybe had something more operable that they could work with, but it was very serious. Her pediatrician and cardiologist told us to go home and come back around seven in the morning. Doctor N, her cardiologist was going to do a cardiac catheterization to ascertain what was wrong and what to do next.

Go home and come back in the morning? Did they really think I was going to sleep? Well, we went home and of course, I was worried sick. Here is my tiny, fragile, little baby girl in the hospital, very sick and I can't do anything to help. I decided that was not acceptable, so I made a list and called everyone I could think of in the morning to ask them to put Heather on their prayer chains at church. I believed in the power of prayer and wanted everyone to send prayers up for Heathers' speedy recovery, from whatever this diagnosis was. Needless to say I didn't sleep at all and I was at the hospital bright and early the next day. When you leave the hospital with your new baby one month and everything is okay, never in a million years do you expect to be told your life could be crushed one month later. I had to get there to see that she was okay in the morning.

When I arrived at the hospital, Heather was sleeping. I thanked God she was okay. She looked like a little angel, so sweet and innocent laying in her hospital bed. Doctor N came into her room and told me he found three problems with Heather's heart when he did the test. She had a very small left ventricle, a hole between her two upper chambers of her heart, and a blockage in her aorta. Heather was sleeping as a result of her tests, and the Dr. said there was really nothing we could do at that time. She would be asleep for quite a while from the anesthesia. We decided to go visit both sets of grandparents to tell them what was happening. While we were at my parent's home, I received a call from Doctor N. He said he assessed that Heather also had a very bad valve in her heart. They wanted to transfer her to

Children's Hospital of Philadelphia for further evaluation right away.

    Children's Hospital of Philadelphia! My mind started turning and running through how I was going to work this out logistically. Heather was taken by ambulance to Children's Hospital of Philadelphia (CHOP) and admitted. I myself, had never been in the hospital for anything, but I did help my mom with my little brother Jim when he was born. He was sick with multiple medical issues. I saw how the illness of Jim affected my mom and I wondered what or how I would handle any crisis with my baby. Mom was great during crisis and then fell apart afterward. I was starting to pray that I could be the same way, so I could be strong for Heather in the present moment. I just couldn't imagine that now this same type of experience was happening again, only this time to my little girl, my own flesh and blood, my first baby.

IN PHILADELPHIA – CHAPTER TWO

Our local Medical Center sent Heather to Children's Hospital of Philadelphia on Tuesday, October the tenth, 1978. She was admitted to CHOP at six thirty in the evening. At our local hospital, I was not allowed to touch her, hold her, or even get very close. The surroundings were very sterile of course and she looked colorless when we left for CHOP. When we got everything taken care of that we had to do upon admission, the nurse came and told me I could come in and see her for a bit. I walked in the NICU and I couldn't find my daughter. I started to panic and ran to the nurse. I was in tears thinking she had not made it to the NICU, where they were going to make her heart issues go away! She spoke very calmly and said why yes, she's right over there. She pointed to this sweet, beautiful little girl in a baby seat, partially sitting up, with pink blankets and a beautiful little knit hat with pink bows. Gosh, I can see her like it was yesterday. She was dressed in a feminine little nighty and almost all of her wires were hidden by her clothing. I stood there for a moment, trying to put everything together in my head; this was Heather! I ran over to her bedside. I stood there and just looked at her with tears streaming down my cheeks. The nurse said Cheryl, you can hold her if you would like. I just couldn't believe how different the unit was in Philadelphia, compared to our local hospital. I was so thankful. I got to hold my daughter, and rock her and cuddle her for quite some time before they said she needed to have a few more blood tests and other things done. And so the journey at CHOP began. Wednesday and Thursday Heather was going to have EKG's and x-rays. They also hooked her up right away to a heart monitor. She was given Digoxin to slow down her heart rate in the hope of giving her heart a chance to rest and become stronger. By Friday, October thirteenth, Heather was taken off her heart monitor and her feeding was increased; which made her feeding three ounces every four hours. CHOP physicians said Heather was doing remarkably well.

I guess I should back up a little. When we got Heather settled in, and we felt sort of comfortable leaving, we realized we had no place to stay. Our Pastor had come down to Philadelphia right behind us and the ambulance. I went to him and said we had to call around and find a place to stay. He said not to worry about it; he had booked a hotel room right across the street from CHOP for us. Actually what he had done is booked a suite so we could all be together. This Pastor, Pastor Charrot, was like no other. He took us under his wing and helped us with everything and anything he could. The suite was huge. My mom and dad came down to CHOP and there was plenty of room for them to stay with us. But, we knew we were running up a big bill and by now we knew we had to stay for an indefinite period of time. One of the nurses told us about "Ronald McDonald House" in Philadelphia. It was a home for parents of very sick children at CHOP. It was the first Ronald McDonald House ever in existence. They gave us directions and told us to take a cab and check it out. We moved over into the Ronald

McDonald House on Friday, October thirteenth. It was so fantastic. Originally the house was a funeral home, so it had a great grand staircase and it looked like something out of a story book. We had a small, but very clean room, a family room where people got together and talked in the evenings, or just sat in silence; whatever worked for each individual. Campbell's provided soups and Coca-Cola provided sodas and juices for free, so if we were short on funds, there was always some type of food being provided for us to eat and drink. We could pay to stay if we had the $5.00/night, but even if we did not, we were welcome. It's very easy for me to look back now and see why and how Ronald McDonald House has grown to be what it is today.

Saturday, October fourteenth and Sunday, October fifteenth CHOP Doctors and nurses continued to stabilize Heather. She was now out of congestive heart failure. She had been in congestive heart failure since Monday, October ninth. Monday, October sixteenth, she had another heart catheterization. The Doctor explained a heart catheterization to us as the process of shooting dye into her bloodstream, to see where her problems were. They discovered she did not have a hole between her two heart chambers. Her left ventricle was a little small, but nothing to be concerned about. They were not sure about a valve in her heart; we would hear more about that in the coming week. The diagnosis always came back the same, Chronic Heart Disease with multiple problems.

We were told if we wanted to go home, this would be a good time. Her cardiologist was going to be taking a look at everything and making some decisions early the next week. So, we left and headed home to Palmyra to do some everyday things, like laundry. I don't know if I did any laundry when we got home because it was so hard to be there without my beautiful little girl. I just sat and cried. My husband had gone to work and I felt so alone. I wasn't sure at this point, if I could even go forward. The phone rang and it was Heathers cardiologist at CHOP. He is ready to give me an update. I wasn't sure if I was ready to hear it, especially since I was alone, but I learned quickly I didn't have any choice in the matter. Right now, the Doctor stated his main concern was with her coarctation (blockage) in her aortic artery. This is what he was going to focus on in the next few hours or days. He said Heather was doped up from her test in the morning. She was given a small amount of morphine and they had a little trouble. She went to sleep so deeply, she forgot to breathe. He assured me she would recover from her test and her morphine. I called later and she had stabilized. She had taken sugar water and her color had improved. Heather was also breathing much better. My phone call with the Doctor was fairly quick, but I was glad. I wasn't sure I could comprehend much more on the call. My state of mind was not even clear to myself at this point. Every now and then I had to pinch myself.

I honestly couldn't believe all of this was happening to me. My life growing up was tough with my dad working very long hours and my little brother being extremely sick. Mom and I had our hands full taking care of Jim almost 24/7. I remember coming home from school, doing my homework and going to bed early, intentionally. I would get up about 2am and walk my brother up and down the hallways to try to get him back to sleep. When that didn't work, I would sit in a rocker beside his bed with my arm and hand through the railing and pat him. We tried anything and everything, but he seemed to always be in pain. Mom and I would take turns because dad got up so early and came home so late. Dad worked hard to make ends meet due to large medical bills. He was self-employed with his father and brother, and medical insurance in those days was a very expensive commodity, especially to the self-employed. My life at home went on with a very ill brother until the time I left home at seventeen to attend college. Now, my own life was staring me in the face. I felt like I had already done all of these things with my brother. The worrying, the caring for, the tears. But I realized it was something I was going to have to face, one way or another. I started to say, okay God, why?

On Tuesday, October seventeenth I called at ten at night to check on Heather. As you can imagine it was so hard knowing she was in Philadelphia and I in Palmyra, two hours away. The nurse told me that earlier during the day she wasn't very alert, but her vital signs were normal. At ten o'clock the nurse told me not to worry and that <u>she's the same old Heather.</u> She was much more awake and everything was back to normal. Wednesday, October eighteenth we left home at ten thirty in the morning to go to Philadelphia to see Heather. The cardiothoracic surgeon, Doctor E, and the cardiologist, Doctor W consulted with Doctor N and they decided to postpone her surgery until a later date. At four o'clock in the evening they; both doctors came in and asked if we would like to take Heather home. What a silly question to ask a mom. However, it did seem like a very scary undertaking after I gave it a couple minutes to sink in. Wednesday night at midnight I started giving her Digoxin, .25cc's. I had to give it to her every twelve hours. She fell asleep at eleven, was awakened for her medicine at midnight and went back to sleep until eight Thursday morning. As you can imagine even though she seemed more back to normal, sleeping for me was difficult, to say the least.

THE THIRD SEASON OF FAMILY LIFE
BACK AT HOME – CHAPTER THREE

Friday, October twentieth Heather had an appointment with her pediatrician, Doctor B. He kept Heathers formula the same and said we could feed her every three hours if she wanted to eat, contrary to what pediatricians at Children Hospital had told us. Heather was twenty inches long and the average was twenty one inches. Her weight was ten pounds eleven and one-half ounces and the average was nine pounds. At her two month visit they would start her series of shots. At three months they will do something about her left foot. It had turned in from her fetal position in the womb. When I left her Drs appointment, I actually had two days, Saturday and Sunday when I didn't have to take her to a Doctor, or drive to Philadelphia. I just wanted to concentrate on spending some wonderful quality time with my little girl that God had blessed me with, but up to this point, I had not really had that opportunity. We didn't really go anywhere, but we spent some special time, mommy reading books, rocking, brushing her curly hair and putting it into tiny little ponytails. It was great mommy Heather time that we both needed very much.

Monday, October twenty third came around so quickly. Heather had an appointment with her cardiologist in Harrisburg, Doctor N. He said everything sounded good, but he <u>is a little worried about her weight</u>. He said to follow her pediatricians order and feed her only formula, every 3 hours if she was hungry. Since she was <u>out of congestive heart failure,</u> and the medicine was working, so her fluid intake was not as much of a problem. Out of congestive heart failure. That statement sang around me like an endless spiral wind chime and the thought of what does it mean, twirled around me just like the wind chime. Little did I know, Heather wouldn't be "out of congestive heart failure" for much of her short little life.

On October twenty seventh I took Heather to the pediatrician's practice. She was vomiting and I was not sure what was going on. Every time Heather got sick, I panicked and wondered what in the world was in store for this little child. I became an overly concerned mommy, but the Doctors seemed to deal with that just fine. They always told me not to hesitate to ask questions and to make sure I understood what they were saying. Heathers care took on a life of its own, but it was one I was definitely willing to take. Her care was 24/7 considering all the things I had to "monitor" in her precious little life. The pediatrician prescribed Pedialyte for twenty four hours, then one-half strength formula for twenty four hours, at the end of which they advised to put her back on regular feedings. She just had a virus, what a relief for me. I was always so thankful every time it was something "normal". It seemed strange to me when friends would call and say, oh Cindy has a virus, she's so sick. Not that I meant to trivialize a virus in another child, but I always had to say Thank you when Heather had a virus. I always tried to sympathize with my friends, but in the back of my mind I was thinking, you're so lucky, please count your blessings for those little viruses.

On November seventh, I noticed Heather was breathing at a rather fast pace. With her care, I had learned to time her respirations, take her blood pressure, listen to her heart, whatever needed to be done. I timed her respirations and they were seventy three. Normal range was forty to sixty. I immediately called Doctor N and he told me to watch her through the night and bring her in to the office the next morning. At nine in the morning, November eighth, we went to Doctor N's office. He said Heather looked good, but that she needed her Digoxin increased a bit from .25cc to .3cc. He also told me that it was not unusual for babies' respiration to be fast for brief periods of time, and not to worry, unless this became an extended observation. He was so patient with me and always explained the how's and why's of every situation. Being a dad himself, I'm sure he sincerely cared deeply about all of his patients. He always showed that extra bit of compassion with Heather. I noticed a lot of specialists; especially surgeons did not show that closeness to their patients. I assumed it's because they're afraid to get close to all of them, especially since these surgeons were the ones who had these children's lives in their hands.

On November twenty seventh, I got Heather all dressed up and we went to see her pediatrician's for her well baby visit. There's a lot of detail following because I was so happy and noted everything for a real "well baby" visit. She was given her first diphtheria, tetanus, and pertussis vaccine, along with an oral poliovirus vaccine. Heather weighed in that day at nine pounds, so the doctor increased her Digoxin again to .04 ccs. The Doctor told me when I took Heather to see her cardiologist on December twentieth; he will probably increase her Digoxin one more time. Her pediatrician also noticed her left foot seemed to be correcting itself. He told me to supplement her formula with only fruit, if necessary, to satisfy her. He gave me nose drops to use every six hours for her congestion she had from time to time. Life went back to normal, as normal as could be, until December 20th when we were preparing for Christmas, but had to take time to go see Heather's cardiologist. The news I heard at this appointment, of possibly moving her surgery up in date, was not what I wanted to hear.

On December twentieth Heather saw her pediatric cardiologist at two o'clock. He was very pleased with her weight, and her EKG looked fine. He increased her Digoxin a tiny bit and changed the dosage to every twelve hours, because of her weight gain. He explained Heathers coarctation further. Since the blockage was before her veins to the arms, and legs, the Doctors were never able to get a pulse in those extremities. This increased the potential of moving her heart surgery up in date. Why? Everything else seemed to look really good. Doctor N was concerned because pressure may make her blood back up into the aorta, as she grew and became more active. Doctor N gave me the okay to give Heather any foods, and we were going to start swimming lessons for her. He said the strain would not hurt her. So, here we are five days before Christmas. Why do they have to move her surgery date up? I heard him, I really did. I understood him, I really did. But still, my heart was saying why do they have to move her surgery date up? I guess I was just being a mom. I got past this appointment and the disappointment of the surgery date change and was looking forward now to Christmas day for Heather.

So, we were ready to celebrate Heather's first Christmas. It was very bittersweet. I was so happy that we were home. Daddy had to work that morning, so we didn't celebrate until evening. But that was okay because Mommy and Heather got to spend a great day together. We talked to Nana and PapPap and decided to go to church with them. I didn't like taking her around people because of all the germs, but I needed to spend time with family on Christmas. And I had bought her an adorable little outfit for Christmas that I wasn't sure if she would get to wear or not. After church, we went to Nana and PapPap's, had lunch and opened presents from Nana and PapPap. After spending some time there, we went home and Heather took a nice nap right up until Daddy got home from work. Of course Santa had come to our house too, so in the evening we opened presents and enjoyed more family time together with Daddy.

On December twenty eighth, I was off with Heather to the pediatricians' office again. She got her second DPT shot and weighed in at ten and one half pounds, and was twenty four inches long. Her feet were windswept from her position in the uterus. This meant both of her feet faced the same position, contrary to the norm. I was given a prescription for corrective shoes which would have a bar between them, to be worn twenty two hours a day, moving to just at night after one month, to maintain the correction. Corrective shoes with a heavy bar between them. Why in the world would this poor little girl have to deal with this yet? Really, isn't her heart problem enough? I felt so sorry for her. Again I asked, why God. Her pediatrician continued and told me he was pleased with her weight and told me to keep her on formula, cereal and fruit; no vegetables or meat as of yet. The protein which she was obtaining from her formula was the most important form of nutrition for her. Her Digoxin dosage stayed the same. This was the second time I sat down and had a serious, very serious conversation with my maker. God, how could this all happen to one little girl, my precious little baby? I didn't care about my stress, her dads stress, the rest of the family or anything else, but HOW could this all happen to one precious little girl. The love of my life. He really didn't have an answer for me, but I continued to have faith that he knew what was right and would direct us all in the right direction. I told myself that someday I would understand all of this.

A NEW YEAR, A NEW BEGINNING
– CHAPTER FOUR

On January eighteenth, Pastor Charrot came to our home to anoint Heather in hopes of healing, or to gain special attention from God. He read James 5:14 and I believe she was healed in some ways, maybe in ways I didn't even know about. James 5:14 New American Standard Bible states: Is anyone among you sick? Then he must call for the elders of the church and they are to pray over him, anointing him with oil in the name of the Lord. He anointed her with the shape of the cross on her forehead and said a blessing and a prayer. I wasn't sure about anything at this point, but I know I wanted my sweet little girl to be healed. I certainly didn't want to lose her. After the anointing, Heather and I spent almost two weeks together and we actually began to have a daily routine, somewhat normal. That in itself was a miracle. We had a time to go to bed, a time to get up, mommy actually started sleeping a little better; things almost felt normal. However, when I walked in her room and saw that tiny, petite little girl sleeping soundly, I always had to count respirations and take her heart rate. It was still more normal than I had felt in a long time. That "normal feeling" even carried through her Doctors visit on January thirty first! Heather was growing up to be not only a pretty little girl, but smart and so very happy. She smiled, and was such a happy little baby.

On that day I took Heather to see her pediatrician. He reviewed her condition and then began to examine her. We had different pediatricians because we went to a "group" practice. Because of this, we always had a discussion as soon as they came in the room.

They wanted to know from me, how I felt about everything. Then they would proceed. He said her weight gain and activity were great, considering her condition. He also said to keep her on formula, fruit and cereals and start her on vegetables. She received her third and final DPT shot. He said he would not have to see Heather again for two months unless any unforeseen difficulties arose. This was the first time I left the Doctors office and I felt like maybe we were starting to pass over some hurdles.

Daily life went on fairly normal in February. She was five months old and starting to really "communicate" with me with movements, smiles, and sounds. Right around Valentine's Day she decided to say Momma for the first time. Wow, what a feeling, when I realized she knew who I was, she identified me with a word. When she cried, smiled, blew bubbles and was looking at me, she knew I was Momma. In the month of Love, my little precious, beautiful girl called me Momma. What could be better? Life was great; until February twenty sixth at seven in the evening. I noticed Heathers respiration to be eighty instead of forty. She had been drinking about four ounces every feeding, for the past three days and seemed very cranky and uncomfortable. Her pediatricians asked me to please bring Heather to the hospital. Her crankiness and feeding problems were from her teething. Plus, her respiration could vary, especially if I was upset, then she would tend to be upset also. Her Digoxin levels were checked and we were sent home with directions to follow, for something that seemed so trivial compared to her heart condition. But trivial at this point in time was a good thing and I was so thankful that it wasn't anything serious.

On March thirtieth, Heather had an appointment at the pediatricians' office. She received her oral polio vaccine, her last dose. They also decided to remove the bar she was wearing between her shoes, for good. Her weight was thirteen pounds, so her pediatrician told me not to drop her bedtime bottle. Now, I was finally hopeful that time would progress pretty normally, at least as normal as it could be. Months went by, Pediatrician appointments, Surgeon appointments, Cardiologist appointments, etc. From March thru May, life was good! Heather was a very happy little girl, a very good baby, I couldn't ask for anything more, except a healthy outlook for her. We read lots of little story books; we brushed her hair and rocked a lot. We played with our puppy, and learned to love baths. We didn't go to Sunday School because of the closeness of all the children and all the little "bugs" that went around. But mommy always taught Heather about Jesus and how much he loved her. I told her that Jesus watched over her always. At bed time she had an angel kneeling, hanging from her crib. We always looked at it and said that little angel would watch over her and keep her safe while she slept. That same little angel would always hang on her hospital bed as well. We had made it to six months and mommy was a very happy mommy. On May fourth she saw the doctor again and he said she was ahead of her age group as far as walking and crawling, but slightly underweight. I started table foods and junior baby foods. On May tenth, Heather saw her cardiologist. Her Digoxin was increased to one cc. He determined that her operation could wait until she was five years of age, unless there were any complications before that age. This was a big blessing because I knew the longer we could wait, the more Heathers heart would be developed and the better her chances of survival of any surgeries. He was very pleased with her growth and weight and how well she was doing with the current dosage of Digoxin she was on. We left that appointment and I was certain this was the beginning of a long break before anything serious again. We still continued to go to many doctors' appointments, as you can imagine, between pediatricians and cardiologists, but that was okay with me.

Well, my plan changed a little bit on June seventeenth. Heather was admitted to the hospital for a heart catheterization. It didn't appear to be anything too serious, but she had been having some troubles and her cardiologist wanted to check things out. Her test was done Wednesday morning at eight thirty and she was back in her room by eleven forty five. Heather didn't get through this catheterization like she did all the rest. This one was very hard on her. She lost approximately 50 cc's of blood. Her heart stopped when the second dye was injected, for one and one half seconds. When her heart stopped,

Doctor. N stopped the test. He said the test had produced some good pictures, so he couldn't see prolonging the test and risking Heathers' life. On Friday, June 20th, she was discharged and I took Heather home. On Sunday, her temperature went up to one hundred three degrees. I was told she had a slight cold and sort throat when I took her home on Sunday, but I was still concerned on Monday, with the fever. I called her pediatrician and he said he would meet us at the hospital for a few tests. Sometimes I felt so bad because I felt like a super overprotective mom. But, this was my first little girl and I didn't want to miss something important that would have a detrimental effect on her. When I got to the hospital, the Doctor had a chest x-ray and some blood work done. After the tests the doctor said to please take her upstairs, because she had pneumonia.

Heather was going to be admitted. She was very sick, and I just didn't understand. Why pneumonia, with everything else? She remained in the hospital for quite some time. Thursday, her cardiologist came in and said Heather needed some "packed red cells". Her counts were down and he felt it would really be a help. The problem with this was as follows. The catheterization showed her heart needed surgery because it was under such stress, for various reasons. It was becoming thick and tired. If they inserted new blood to increase the count, it would mess up her pure blood for cross reference if it was necessary to do surgery. We spoke with her physician at CHOP about surgery. He wanted her to have a chest x-ray to check on her pneumonia and he also wanted to know if her culture results had come back. It looked like it was going to be a very hectic day. Days and nights rolled into one during this time. When I was in the hospital, of course it was as if I was outside. All the bright lights and everyone moving about made every moment daytime. Heather and I would spend whatever time I was in there with her reading, telling stories about the day, playing little games, singing songs together. Every moment I had to spend with her was like a gift and I wasn't about to waste any of it.

Friday, I got to the hospital early in the morning. I made it in time to take Heather to her chest x-ray. It was determined after the x-ray; her surgery would be early in June at CHOP, unless any other complications arose. I left the hospital at two thirty to take a minute to digest everything. I returned about five thirty in the evening. Heather was tied to the bed by her legs. An IV and splint were attached to her right leg because they gave her "packed red blood cells". Just what a mom wants to see when they walk in the room, their precious baby tied to the bed by their legs. I know it had to be done that way so she wouldn't injure herself, but it looks so barbaric! I tried to remain calm, once again. Breathe, breathe I kept telling myself. They had to retest her hemoglobin and determine whether or not she needed additional cells. Also, her chest x-ray showed small signs of pneumonia again. On Saturday, June twenty eighth I received a call from her pediatrician. He said Heather was ready for discharge if her blood counts were still okay. They would keep her on an antibiotic until she would go to CHOP in Philadelphia on the eighth of July for her surgery. Her blood tests came back looking good, so we were discharged in the early afternoon of June twenty eighth. Well, we had a week or so until we had to be at CHOP, so Heather and I did a lot of running around, fun things. We went to the swimming pool, HersheyPark, shopping (she loved to shop), and just spent Mommy, Heather time together. I knew surgery was coming up and it was important for me to stay as calm as possible to enable her to remain unstressed. It was so hard, sometimes I had to just sit down and tell myself, it's normal to be upset, stressed, but don't let it show around Heather. Cry if you want, but cry in your pillow at night, not now, not when we're having a great time and I could see she was clearly having fun and smiling. I started thinking, it just isn't fair!

SECOND CHAPTER AT CHILDRENS HOSPITAL IN PHILADELPHIA – CHAPTER FIVE

On July eighth, Heather was admitted to CHOP. We went right to the heart station for her EKG and then on to admissions for lab work. A room was ready for her on the fifth floor, as soon as we arrived. They said tomorrow would be a waiting day to make sure everything checked out okay before the surgery. From this day forward, this hospital stay would become a large whirlwind that we were stuck in. It started when we were leaving the hospital that same day, we ran into one of Heathers physicians. He stated her chest x-ray was cloudy, and her white blood count was elevated. They did not know at this point what would become of her surgery. As you can imagine, the next day they decided to do more tests because in addition to everything else, the surgeon didn't like the sound of her murmur. He said it was likely she had additional heart problems, but she would probably still have her first surgery at this time. Later that day, the anesthesiologist came in and explained all the risks. He was not happy that her pneumonia was only about two weeks earlier. Normally they would wait four weeks after pneumonia to do surgery. However, Heathers cardiologist and cardiothoracic surgeon determined the surgery needed to be done right away. They stated the risk of this surgery was not only death, but paralysis. During the surgery the blood flow had to be shut off to the lower portion of her body and her spinal cord. In order to do this, they lowered her body temperature. This would minimize the risk of paralysis. While the surgeon was with us, he explained that Heather had many other problems. He said at least two valves weren't functioning properly and that the arteries to her arms and the rest of her circulatory system were smaller than normal. This would be part of the reason she was such a tiny, petite little girl. He reminded us of the seriousness and risk associated with the surgery, but stated we really didn't have any other option and time was not on our side.

My mom had bought the little angel kneeling on a cross that always went in the hospital with Heather. She always wanted it tied to the head end of her bed because she knew I told her that the angel would watch over her and keep her safe during the night.

Tonight was no different. When she was ready to go downstairs, she asked if she could please have her angel on the bed with her, so they told her yes and then the nurses would take it off once she was under anesthesia. Oh God, tonight was one of those nights when all I did was pray all night long. I think at this point I realized if I would not have had my faith to fall back on, I don't know what I would have done. Even though faith is believing in something you can't see, you have to believe and concentrate on something with more power than yourself when you're in that situation. Our minds, at least my mind just couldn't wrap itself around everything that was going on. I had to pray just for strength to make it through the next few hours, days, weeks, but mostly the next few seconds.

At five am the next morning, Heather was in the operating room being prepped for surgery. She was already under anesthesia and being prepared for her IV's. At seven o'clock, the nurse informed us that everything was going smoothly, and they were in the area of the aorta. At eight thirty, Heathers surgeon came out and informed us that the operation went well. She had appeared to move her feet, so no paralysis was anticipated. Around nine o'clock we were able to see her in the intensive care unit. I can't even begin to tell you how things looked when we entered the intensive care unit. She was hooked to so many machines, and tubes coming out of her body at so many places, I could hardly see my precious daughter. It's not something a mom ever dreams they will see; especially connected to their own child. It was very overwhelming, but I held it together for

Heathers sake. The doctors explained that without this surgery to remove the coarctation, Heather would most likely have become paralyzed due to a shut off of blood to her spine. She was removed from the respirator about twelve thirty and was breathing on her own with forty percent oxygen.

Again, the surgeons and nurses told me, go home and get some rest. I know they meant well, but... The next day, I went in to see Heather. She was still on twenty five percent oxygen, but other than that, everything seemed to be very good. I knew in my heart, that little angel and cross attached to her bed had definitely watched over her and kept her safe and sound. She was crying and wanted to go home, but of course no one goes home directly from the intensive care unit. They anticipated taking her chest tube out in the morning. At that time I actually got to hold my beautiful child for about ten minutes. She had a lot of bruising and aches and pains, but she was in my arms and awake. What more could I ask for. Sunday was a great day! We went to the playroom and for a buggy ride to McDonalds on the first floor of the hospital. French fries were her favorite and the doctors said go for it. While we were in the hospital this time, Heather and I made lots of friends. We met Jeremy who was born with some very serious health issues that the Doctors were trying to correct. He was born without his male genetalia and they were going to attempt to make parts for Jeremy from a finger and other grafts from other areas of his body. They explained to us that the Doctors were hopeful they would be able to make everything work and eventually Jeremy would be able to have a family and lead a normal life! We also met Cynthia who was also born with her body not exactly correct. Her abdominal body parts were on the outside of her body and her torso was not closed since birth. She was a sweetie pie and Heather and Cynthia became good little friends in the hospital. These two young children, both around Heathers age were in serious situations also. Then there was John. John was a little boy about fourteen months old that was dropped off at the hospital with an eating disorder. He was unable to take anything by mouth. He was fed only through a tube straight into his stomach. It was hard to explain to the other little children. The really sad thing about John is when he was dropped off, he was literally dropped off. No one ever came back for him. Everyone at the hospital sort of "adopted" him while he was in the unit and he was the most cheerful, happy little boy. He bounced around his crib and talked and smiled at everyone that went by or came into the Unit. How sad that someone would leave their child. But then I started thinking, with all the care this little boy took, perhaps his family could not afford to take care of him. Maybe they thought it was best for him. Life takes such bizarre turns for so many people and it's so important not to just rush to judgment about why or how things are happening. I just continued to talk and play with him whenever I was on the Unit, as did most everyone else that went by his crib. He didn't know any better and to John, everything was good and he was so happy!

Thank God Heather was discharged from CHOP on July sixteenth. It was great, I felt like another hurdle was passed. On the eleventh of August, we went to a follow up exam with the surgeon. He said he was very pleased with her development, but he also wanted us to know there was a chance she had cardiomyopathy. This was a disease that affects the muscle of the heart. Prior to birth, it seemed the muscle on the left side of the heart, never developed properly and therefore didn't work properly. They felt in addition to some other things, she had sub-aortic stenosis on the interior of her heart as well.

Everything went along pretty well for about two weeks. Thursday, August eighth Heather's surgeon called and said the results of her holter monitor from the past forty eight hours showed something very serious was wrong again. He said there were several instances where her heart rate dropped to twenty beats per minute or less, and that rate would render her unconscious. He asked me to take her pulse and call him back. Her pulse was okay and doctor was cautious but approving as of that day. Starting in August, Heather and I were attached at the hip. We started having fun and enjoying each other to the fullest.

The Doctors said her IQ was pretty high, which I already knew. She was so smart, so knowledgeable about anything and everything we had taught her. She was two now, but her mental IQ was that of an eight year old little girl. Beautiful, smart, sweet and such a gift. Heather and I did so much running around and making up for time we were unable to spend together in the months before. One day we decided to go to Boscov's to shop. I wanted to get a few things for her and myself for the winter months.

She got cold so easily, so I thought I would look for long underwear for her. It was tough to find because all the spring things were already out. I went from department to department. But, she was a shopper and LOVED looking at everything. Of course we ended up in the department with beautiful little dresses in it. Heather saw a dress she absolutely fell in love with. <u>Mommy, can I have it, Mommy can I have it?</u> Well, how in the world could I say no? So, we went to the ladies lingerie dressing room, so we could grab a little slip to go with the dress. There was a wonderful lady in the lingerie department. I believe her name was Marion. She came right over to Heather and asked her if she could use some help. Of course Heather told her right away that she wanted to try the dress on. The attendant got her a full slip, and helped her put on this beautiful Polly Flinders smocked dress. She danced around the dressing room and was so excited. We decided at that moment, the dress would be her Easter dress. She was so proud of herself. We bought the dress, and the slip and the woman at Boscov's told me how precious she thought Heather was. She said she was so excited to put on this pretty dress and slip and show her mommy. She said you must really be close to your daughter, that's so nice to see. Little did she know Heather was so seriously ill. And I thought to myself; how anyone could not love this little girl, just look at her. I'm so thankful that she made her "shopping experience" so special!

Everything went along pretty smoothly until November twentieth. This was a welcome change for both Heather and I, not running back and forth from hospitals to home for a couple weeks. Heather was at her daycare, which she loved, and I received a call that she had a spell of falling, turning pale, panting and complained of pain. I rushed to the sitters' home and took her directly to her cardiologist. He said I should hope she had a correctable type of myopathy, sub aortic stenosis. If it wasn't that, it was some type of myopathy and he was not too sure what they could do. On November twenty first Heather had another spell. Her cardiologist was alerted and he continued to monitor her by attaching a holter monitor and ran it for a twenty four hour period. The next three days in November seemed to pass without a hitch. The doctor was going to do another catheterization on the twenty sixth, however he wanted to put her under anesthesia because of her reaction to the last catheterization. One morning in the hospital, prior to the day of her catheterization, I went in and was met by a Med Student. He said he wanted to chat and learn more about Heather and what was going on. No problem, I understand the students had to learn. So, we chatted for quite some time. At the end of the conversation, he stood up and told me he felt this condition that was showing up was not heart related. He was certain that Heather was throwing temper tantrums and that's why she was falling. I stood up and looked at this young student and said what??? Of course she's not throwing temper tantrums. She does not have that type of temperament. She is very calm, cool and collected and a sweet child that had never thrown any type of tantrum. He continued to argue with me that this was not a heart related condition at all. For a split second I wanted to believe him that it was not heart related, but I knew, Heather was not the type of child to throw a tantrum. Unknown to me, Dr. Nordenberg walked through the doorway while the student was arguing with me. He took the student by the coat collar and said, <u>don't ever let me see you arguing with a mother again. If anyone knows their child better than anyone else, it's a mother. Especially this mother,</u> he said. He knew how much time and devotion I had put into this little precious girls life and that I would know if she was throwing temper tantrums. We had the best Doctors one could ask for. The Med student apologized to me and that was the last time I saw him.

On Thanksgiving Day, November twenty seventh, Heather was recuperating from her catheterization. Her results weren't too good. Her aortic arch was very sharp and it took two hours to enter the groin, get around the arch and enter the valve. The doctor was only able to get one picture but he said that one was very good. Heather turned pale and didn't look good, so Doctor N decided to stop the cath. They needed to be able to complete the test, so he stated that they were going to try again, but to use a very skinny catheter, on Monday. The doctor sat us down and said Heather has a <u>very serious and unique problem</u>, and he would not send her home until it was resolved. My life was just horrible right now, horrible. I didn't know what to do. My faith was running slim and I felt like prayers and God and everyone was forgetting me, forgetting Heather. How in the world could I go on without someone's help? Scared doesn't begin to describe my feelings. I felt like all of my worst nightmares were coming together and I wasn't going to wake up from them. My poor baby girl, to look at her all you thought was, she's tiny. But, that's not the truth, inside that precious little girl was so sick, so very sick. This just couldn't be happening. I tried to convince myself that this must be wrong, everything would change. I just didn't know what to do.

On December first she was having her second catheterization. It went well and the doctor got the pictures that he needed. The news was not good. It seemed that Heather did have sub valvulor stenosis, but the left ventricle was also very sluggish. We were now faced with a must; open heart surgery. The risk of the surgery was great, but without it she didn't have a chance. On December second, Heathers pediatrician came in to see us and to make sure we fully understood the situation. He was the first doctor to use the term endocardiofibrolastosis. Heather had two blockages one under the aortic valve, and one under the mitral valve. Also, her left ventricle was sluggish and being strangled by the blockages. What we learned at that time was mind boggling. For two years we had been giving her Digoxin, which is good for the bad ventricle, but bad for the blockages. Christmas Day, December twenty fifth at twelve o'clock, Heather was admitted again to the hospital. This time she had three spells where she got very rigid, closed her eyes and stopped breathing. These spells were very scary to say the least. At this point, the doctors felt she was having some type of seizures, but they weren't sure if it was heart related or not. As of December twenty sixth, I just couldn't believe this poor child had to go through something else, for this new problem. On the twenty seventh, she was doing fairly well, but was not eating anything. On the twenty eighth of December, it seemed Heather had turned a corner and was doing pretty well. She was eating, her EKG was fine and she was scheduled for an EEG. A pediatric neurologist would be coming to speak with us after the EEG.

The pediatric neurologist said he needed to put her on something for the seizures. He also had sent her tests and pictures to a baby hospital in New York, where he would get a second opinion. After he received the opinion, we were told without the heart surgery <u>she would not be with us for very many years</u>. Those words stayed with me forever. Even today I can remember when he said them and exactly how I felt. This Doctor had this all wrong. I didn't have this beautiful baby girl to give her up. I wanted to watch her grow up, go to school and get married. I was sure that was the case, no matter what this Doctor was telling me. How dare he tell me that! On December twenty ninth, Heather went for her EEG. The results were good and her Neurologist also reconfirmed that Heather had the intelligence level of approximately an eight year old child. I asked to speak with Heather's cardiologist at this time. Her dad and I explained how much she loved Minnie Mouse, which he already knew. I asked if it would be safe to take her to Disneyworld. He explained to us that as a physician, he would say no. As a father, he would say yes, go for the trip. Dr. Nordenberg said he would provide us with numbers for a cardiac contact in Orlando as well as have a Medical transport ready to bring her home if need be. The decision was made. She was discharged at that time with no real answers. Now, back in these days, there was no "Make-A-Wish" or any such thing, so we charged everything. We ran up two charge cards, getting hotel rooms on the grounds so she could rest when need be, flights, food, clothing, etc. Almost immediately when we left the hospital, we got everything together and headed to Orlando. Time stood still. She got to meet Minnie Mouse, Mickey Mouse, we had an autograph book that they signed, and we had breakfast, lunch and dinner with them. It was amazing how quickly they got from one side of the park to the other. Heather said it was "magic". I guess she was right since we were in the "Magic Kingdom". I wish I could tell you how magical the trip was to me. It was sad, I had moments where I would just cry and cry, when she wasn't aware of course. I felt like it was the last trip I would ever be able to take her on. Then there were moments of pure joy watching her play and talk with Minnie and Mickey. She was so happy.

Little did I know the trip to Disneyworld at the end of December, with all the magic would now become the terror and fear of March. On March first, Heather woke up screaming. She looked like a child in extreme heart failure. By now, I had known what heart failure looked like in my little two year old girl. She was white as the sheets, her lips and face were also white. She was crying and couldn't keep her eyes open. She also pointed to her heart and said her boo boo was hurting. I called the ambulance and a good friend who was a driver for the ambulance company. We went to the hospital in record time. Heathers cardiologist admitted her as quickly as possible and got started with tests. March second started out very normal. However, during the day she had several very bad seizures. She was getting so pale and having the seizures closer and closer together. Her cardiologist came in towards evening and said he truly did not know the cause of the seizures. He started a new drug therapy with Heather, hoping to get her heart back to beating consistently. Later that same evening, she had more episodes and each seemed to get progressively worse. She stopped breathing and we were rushed out of the room. Around midnight, she was transferred back to the intensive care unit. She had twelve spells in a twenty four hour period.

On March fourth, I arrived about eleven o'clock. Heather had three spells and she was really tired. She had another right after I got there and her cardiologist caught some of it. He said he felt pretty certain that this was her heart and that something would have to be done very soon. They put an IV in her foot, just in case they had to give her Heparin quickly. The next day, March fifth, Heather was transferred to five Med at CHOP. The docs there were going to do a team conference about Heather and were deciding what to do next. After two seizures, one right after the other, they gave her oxygen and did an EKG right away. Heather remained in five Med. It was awful. For two days I sat and waited and waited. It seemed like a lifetime, watching her have seizures and knowing I couldn't do anything about them and praying the Doctors would know what to do.

Finally, we met with the cardiothoracic surgeon on March seventh. He decided he was going to review everything and let us know the next day what had to be done. Since we had arrived, Heather seemed to be doing fair. I stayed with her round the clock, whenever I could. There was no way I was going to let her there knowing how much she was hurting and how tired and exhausted she had become.

On Sunday morning, March eighth, her team of doctors came in and explained the possibilities we had for surgery. They explained that once they were inside her heart, they would decide which of the three procedures they would use. They explained every one to us in very great detail. They also explained whatever procedure they did, Heather would have to go for blood work every two weeks for the rest of her life. Little did we know, the rest of her life, would only be days.

CLOSING IN --- CHAPTER SIX

Around ten pm, an anesthesiologist came in and explained the risk involved with the surgery again. The next morning, March ninth, Heather received two shots in her legs about seven thirty in the morning. One shot was to make her sleepy; the other was to rid her of any additional moisture in her body. We went down to the hallway outside the surgical suite. Something I've not mentioned in this book, that I need to tell you now. Heather loved Minnie Mouse so much that she always had her mouse with her. She also had her angel kneeling in prayer tied to her crib every time we were in the hospital. As my precious little girl lay in her crib, getting drowsier and drowsier, she looked up at me and said, <u>Mommy, will I see Jesus?</u> I told her no, I didn't think so. It wasn't time yet. At about eight thirty, they took Heather into the "holding room" for surgery. Now I could finally breathe and cry. That's all I did for the next day or so. We received a report about ten thirty saying that Heather was totally under and asleep, but that they were still running IV lines. At noon, they were still running lines. They finished putting in all lines right after noon and at one o'clock, her cardiologist informed us that Heather was on the heart lung machine. At three, her cardiothoracic surgeon came to us and said the operation was basically finished, and that in about one-half hour they would start weaning her from the heart/lung machine.

At quarter of five, the surgeon came out and said they were cautiously optimistic about her recovery.

He stated she was off the heart/lung machine and the heart was beating on its own. Finally, I felt like my prayers had been answered, that someone had been listening, that my baby girl would be back in my arms again, and that we could do ponytails and story books and sing together again.

The Doctor came out and said Heathers chest had not been closed yet, because they needed to monitor her closely and make sure her heart continued to work properly. At six o'clock that evening things started to change.

Her heart had stopped and they had to massage her heart for ten minutes, until they could get her back on the heart/lung machine. They continued to monitor her in the operating room, till about nine o'clock when they transported her to intensive care unit. The surgeon informed us things were not good. In fact, they were very critical. There was some trouble with her kidneys, she was bleeding badly, and there was a possibility of brain damage when she had her set back. In the wee hours of the morning, we realized that Heather might not make pull through this. Two of her attending team members, stayed with her through the night and came out and talked to us when they could. They said everything seemed to be changing second by second. The medicine they gave her for her heart was hurting her kidneys, and vice versa. Things didn't look good; whatever they attempted seemed to affect another area of the body, in a bad way. Heather was put on a dialysis machine to try to help the kidneys and drain some of the fluids in her chest. She starting losing a lot of blood and the Doctors really felt we were losing her.

By morning, she was holding her own. The surgeon said it was in his words, <u>a miracle that she is still with us</u>. Her blood was not clotting during the night, but now appeared to be clotting. They had to get the central venus line out of her neck or there would be a possibility of a stroke. At ten thirty, her blood loss was very small, but her blood was not clotting as they had thought. One of the medications they were giving her was constricting the blood vessels in her extremities, and that was a major concern as well. Her blood pressure went up and down. She coded several times, but they were always able to revive her.

Around noon, we were surrounded by friends and family and our Pastor, our real rock during this whole ordeal. Pastor Charrot thought it would be a good idea for us to pray. Only he said we should not be praying for our will be to be done, but <u>thy will be done</u>. I went in to Heather on one of my visits around twelve thirty by myself. We were told to talk with her because they understood she may be able to hear and comprehend. No one really knew. So, I did. I sat down and took the hand of this little girl I loved so very much. During my prayers and talks with her, I told her if she would come home for Easter, I would get her a bunny that she wanted, a real bunny. Before I left her side, for what I did not know would be the last time, the doctor came over and put his arm around me. He said talk to her, don't stop talking to her. I saw a tear run down his cheek. I asked Heather if she could hear me, to please squeeze my hand. She squeezed my hand. At twelve forty five, the afternoon of March tenth, nineteenth eighty one, Heather Ann Wolf passed away. Cause of death was congenital heart disease. Heather was two years, six months and one day, at the time of her death. Heather was buried the morning of March thirteenth, which was a Friday. Somehow the meaning of Friday the thirteenth had changed dramatically for me that day.

We went home the day she passed away with our Pastor. I'm not sure how our car got home, but I know we did not drive home. People deal with the death of a child in many different ways. It was a very tough time. One would hope that everything would go smoothly during this very awful time. As if death isn't hard enough, my mother-in-law decided to come and kneel down in front of me right after we found out she had died. She said, honey your pastor is coming in between our family. She and my father-in-law wanted to take us home. I was not very close to my in-laws and felt I needed to be with my Pastor at that time. After that situation with my then in-laws, Heathers surgeon Dr. Wagner called us into his office to discuss an autopsy. I immediately said no! He then explained that the rare conditions that Heather had would really help them to learn more about heart disease in children. He asked if I would sign for a partial autopsy, just of her heart. After much thought and many tears I agreed to the partial autopsy, and signed for just the autopsy of her heart. The surgeon then asked me if I was planning to have any additional children or if I was only planning to have one. I said I had always wanted two children, but the possibility of me having another was slim. Dr. Wagner looked me in the eye, this man that I thought was cold and callous and with a tear in his eye, he said Cheryl, please have another child. You are an excellent mother and I would hate to see you not have the experience of raising another child. He said the chance of having another child with heart disease definitely increases after the first with heart disease, but that he would strongly encourage me to move forward with a family when I was ready. I knew at that moment, that would take a lot of thought and understanding on my part before I was ready.

We left CHOP and of course had to go right to the Funeral home. We went to a local funeral home and were greeted at the door. My dad had contacted them and told them we would be coming. The man that helped us at the Funeral home was not nice. He immediately asked if we had signed for an autopsy. I said I didn't want to, but that the surgeon said if they just autopsy her heart, it may help another child, so I agreed to just a heart autopsy. The Funeral home attendant went off the deep end and told me they never know how the bodies will come back after any type of autopsy. He was hoping <u>they wouldn't cut up the body too much</u>. It was the most awful experience of my life. I had to go right from that to picking out her casket. Another horrible experience. A little tiny casket is so different than an adult casket and no one should be choosing a child's casket, especially not the child's parents.

Clothing, what in the world would I do about a special dress for Heather? I couldn't sleep worrying about how I would buy one without her. I couldn't go without her, she loved to shop.

Then I remembered. She and I bought her special dress at Boscov's and were saving it for Easter. She never got to wear it. I had the perfect dress, and Heather had picked it out.

Heather was buried in that beautiful little Polly Flinders dress. She died before Easter. After she passed away, I received a note from the attendant at the Boscov's store. She said she really didn't know us, but that she had helped Heather try on the pretty dress and full slip and she knew it had to be our Heather. She told me how Heather had touched her life that day. My baby was such a special child. She had touched so many people in all different ways. I still couldn't understand why all of this was happening. My maker and I had another discussion and I knew that a day would come that would bring me back to this time and place and I would understand what to do and how to do whatever it was. He obviously had a better plan for Heather than I could ever have had.

Several weeks after I lost her, I received bills from the hospitals totaling $38,000.00 and $52,000.00 and radiologic bills that were way above $150,000.00, plus we received all the charge bills that took years to pay off. Things just weren't looking up anytime soon.

The only plus side to all the bills were the charge bills to Disney. They are the best memories of my entire life so far and that was many years ago. I am so very glad to this day that I wrote a journal of my life with Heather from the day she was born. Why, you might ask? I'm not sure why I started it, but I'm glad I have it. People think they remember things well, but even though I slept, dreamt, ate, walked, talked and breathed my life for two years six months and one day with Heather, every detail is forever etched in my mind even more precisely when I read the journal and trust me, I will never stop. People say, wow that must have been awful, but I always respond with no, she was the best thing that ever happened to me. If I had it to do all over again, I would. There is no doubt in my mind. I learned a lot about life during that time, how precious it is. How foolish we are to worry about stupid little things, or even stupid big things. All the energy and stress we use and put on our bodies. Our body that is so precious. We need to learn to love those around us, whether or not they understand why or how and if they don't accept us, move on because life is definitely too short to worry. Just because some people, some family too, don't show their love for us doesn't mean we can't still love them. Love those who want to be loved also. They will love you back. Be true to our own hearts because our hearts are very fragile things. And they can stop at any moment.

I was very blessed and had a beautiful healthy son Aaron after the death of Heather, and then I had a beautiful healthy daughter Sara. Sara has a beautiful career and a nice husband, George and they have given us a beautiful grandson, Damian. But, even having said that, for thirty years, I never understood how or why a child as special as Heather would be taken from me.

Losing a child was something I never thought I would go through, no one ever expects it. However, somehow I knew, after a couple of months, that I would be okay, someday. There must have been a higher power that needed her for something very special.

Heathers grandpa offered to buy her a headstone, but it just wasn't the right one. I knew the one I wanted was going to be expensive, but I didn't care. I wasn't able to give Heather the real bunny I had promised her, but I finally found a headstone with a little girl with flowers in her hair, and a bunny by her side and it was perfect for my little angel. I decided since it was my gift to her, I would pay for it. We were fortunate that my mother and father had cemetery plots that were not going to be used, so they gave us a plot that we could use. Thank Goodness because at this point, we were drowning in debt. After we buried Heather and the headstone was placed, I realized I was being prepared when my little girl looked up at me and asked <u>Mommy, will I see Jesus?</u> She knew and she was letting me know that she would indeed see Jesus and that everything would be alright.

A NEW CHAPTER IN MY LIFE
– CHAPTER SEVEN

My life kept having a lot of interesting turns after Heather passed. My mother became ill with Lewis Body Syndrome and Parkinson's disease. They are both ugly diseases that encompass Dementia. If you have lived with anyone you love having any type of dementia you will know that it's an awful disease. My mom was very close to Heather and took her death very hard. She also had a daughter she lost at birth. She confided in me that losing Heather was almost like losing her own child. Mom always said Heather was very special, and indeed mom was right. My mom ended up in a very nice nursing facility and every time I went to visit, I realized I was losing a second very close loved one in my life. My mom passed in away in 2005, without really knowing who I was anymore. My brother became ill again and continues to be sick with Congestive Heart Disease. My son became ill with MS like symptoms. My daughter has RSD as does her husband. They say God doesn't give one any more than they can handle. Sometimes I look up and say, <u>Really, I don't need any more</u>. However, I'm not the one that makes that decision. In 2002 I got divorced. Losing someone changes us, but losing a child changes more than we can imagine. I really think bitterness played a part in the demise of my first marriage. They say parents either come together or work apart. Two more children after Heather and there were big changes going on in my marriage. We were definitely coming apart. Many, many different factors, but I'm sure the death of Heather, even though it was many years later, did have an impact on things. It's a life changing event that stays with you forever and ever. Trust me.

I was so extremely happy when Bob passed my way at my place of work. We immediately had a connection in so many ways, but the major one was our love of the water. The water gives us both a sense of peace and calming; a strong connection with each other too. The water seems to be a very strong lifeline for both of us. Being on the water with Bob gave me a renewed sense of being. My new mother and father in law are also water lovers. I believe God has me in the right place once again. For some reason my connection with my in-laws is stronger than I ever thought it could be. Right now I am once again surrounded by people I love, and that love me back. What more could I ask for than to help others who have gone through similar life experiences as myself. I don't want anything back from my experiences, I want to give. They say life is a gift, so I thought, let me give it to others.

In 2011, my soul mate and second husband Bob and I were sitting in our boat on the Susquehanna River in Pennsylvania. The winds were calm, the river almost like a lake, flat with a few ripples, the sun shone bright. Bob said <u>it doesn't get any better than this. Cheryl, you know what I would like to do? I would like start a group to take kids and their families out on the water. Youth who have been ill or are disadvantaged, and need a break from life. If only</u>

<u>for a few hours, just to relax, not worry about anything, just be free</u>……Thus a new chapter in my life began. I told Bob the most important thing to me would be to have these trips at no cost to the families. Bob and I began our 501(c) (3), <u>Captains Sharing & Caring</u> in 2011.

After all the bills I had incurred for two and one half years of my life with my first husband; Bob had hit the nail on the head. I said, <u>great, let's do this</u>. I think at first Bob thought we were crazy to even embark on something so big, but I knew together we could do it. We worked very hard on our 501(c) (3) and acquired it very quickly, in less than six months. We then started our journey on the Chesapeake Bay. We have children and their families from all over Pennsylvania and Maryland that join in our trips. We also have wonderful volunteer captains and clubs that host and help us provide a great day for the families. Of course a lot of volunteers in many capacities make up our group. And, ninety nine percent of them say to us after a trip. <u>I don't know who got more out of that, the family or me.</u> It is a very rewarding experience, and we're doing something for people at no cost to them. I know how important the no cost portion is, from my own life experience. We work solely on donations. I am proud to say that this summer 2014; we collaborated with Bush River Yacht Club on the Chesapeake Bay, Norman Creek Marina and several other marinas and private homes. We were able to sponsor a very special family for Christmas of 2013. They were so thankful and it was just one more way we can give back to others. We are hopeful that we can sponsor a much deserving family this Christmas of 2014 as well. My angel, Heather, is gone from her physical life, but she's with me on every trip. She clears the clouds for us and I feel her presence every moment on the trip.

So as you can see, it took me thirty years to figure out why or how Heather could be taken from me, but I know now she has my hand as I did hers, moving forward. She is helping me, help other families do special things with their loved ones, just in case that day comes when they are not able to do so anymore. She definitely has my hand.

www.ingramcontent.com/pod-product-compliance
Lightning Source LLC
Chambersburg PA
CBHW032019040426
42448CB00006B/662